LUCENT LIBRARY OF
BLACK HISTORY

AFRICAN AMERICANS
IN THE ARMED FORCES

By Tamra B. Orr

Portions of this book originally appeared in
Fighting for Freedom: Blacks in the American Military by Gail B. Stewart.

LUCENT
P R E S S

Published in 2020 by
Lucent Press, an Imprint of Greenhaven Publishing, LLC
353 3rd Avenue
Suite 255
New York, NY 10010

Designer: Deanna Paternostro
Editor: Diane Bailey

Library of Congress Cataloging-in-Publication Data

Names: Orr, Tamra, author.
Title: African Americans in the armed forces / Tamra B. Orr.
Description: New York : Lucent Press, [2020] | Series: Lucent library of
  black history | Includes bibliographical references and index.
Identifiers: LCCN 2019018270 (print) | LCCN 2019021180 (ebook) | ISBN
  9781534568518 (eBook) | ISBN 9781534568501 (library bound book) | ISBN
  9781534568495 (pbk. book)
Subjects: LCSH: United States–Armed Forces–African Americans. | African
  American soldiers–History.
Classification: LCC E185.63 (ebook) | LCC E185.63 .O763 2020 (print) | DDC
  355.0089/96073–dc23
LC record available at https://lccn.loc.gov/2019018270

Printed in China

Some of the images in this book illustrate individuals who are models. The depictions do not imply
actual situations or events.

CPSIA compliance information: Batch #BW20KL: For further information contact Greenhaven Publishing LLC, New York, New York at 1-844-317-7404.

Please visit our website, www.greenhavenpublishing.com. For a free color catalog of all our
high-quality books, call toll free 1-844-317-7404 or fax 1-844-317-7405.

CONTENTS

FOREWORD

From medicine and law to sports and literature, African Americans have played a major role in the history of the United States. However, these groundbreaking men and women often faced prejudice and persecution. More than 300 years ago, Africans were taken in chains from their home and enslaved to work for the earliest American settlers. They suffered for more than two centuries under the brutal oppression of their owners until the outbreak of the American Civil War in 1861. After the dust settled four years later and thousands of Americans—both black and white—had died in combat, slavery in the United States had been legally abolished. By the turn of the 20th century, with the help of the 13th, 14th, and 15th Amendments to the U.S. Constitution, African American men had finally won significant battles for the basic rights of citizenship, but the fight for equality was far from over. Even after the successes of the civil rights movement, the struggle continued—and it still continues today.

Although the history of the African American experience is not always a pleasant story, it is also filled with powerful moments of positive change. These triumphs of human equality were achieved with help from brave social activists such as Frederick Douglass, Martin Luther King Jr., and Maya Angelou. They all experienced racial prejudice in their lifetimes and fought by writing, speaking, and acting against it. By exposing the suffering of the black community, they brought people together to try to remedy centuries' worth of wrongdoing.

Today, it is important to learn about the history of African Americans and their experiences in modern America in order to work toward healing the divide that still exists in the United States. This series aims to give readers a deeper appreciation for and understanding of a part of the American story that is often left untold.

Even before the legal emancipation of slaves, black culture was thriving despite many attempts to suppress it. From music to language to art, slaves began cultivating an identity that was completely unique. Soon after these slaves were granted citizenship, African American culture burst into the mainstream. New generations of authors, scholars, painters, and singers were born, and they spread an appreciation for black culture across America and the entire world. Studying the contributions of these talented individuals fosters a sense of optimism. Despite the cruel treatment and racist attitudes these men and women faced, they never gave up, and they helped change the world with their determination and unique voices.

The Lucent Library of Black History offers a glimpse into the lives and accomplishments of some of the most important and influential African Americans across historical time periods and areas of interest. From the arts and sports to the military and politics, the wide variety of topics allows readers to get a full and clear picture of the successes and struggles African Americans have experienced and are continuing to experience. Titles examine primary source documents and quotes from historical and modern figures to provide an enriching learning experience for readers. With detailed timelines, unique sidebars, and a carefully selected bibliography for further research, this series gives readers the tools to independently discover historical events and figures that do not often get their time in the spotlight.

By balancing the harsh realities of the past and present with a sense of hopefulness for the future, the Lucent Library of Black History helps young people understand an essential truth: Black history is a vital part of American history.

SETTING THE SCENE:

1866
African American soldiers serving with the 10th Cavalry Regiment of the U.S. Army earn the nickname "buffalo soldiers," a term later extended to black soldiers in general.

1917–1918
African American troops fight during World War I in Europe, where they often receive better treatment than in the United States.

1775–1783
African Americans fight in the Ameican Revolution, helping America win freedom from Britain.

| 1775–1783 | 1861 | 1863 | 1866 | 1917–1918 | 1919 |

1863
President Abraham Lincoln signs the Emancipation Proclamation, setting slaves free in the Confederacy and formally allowing African Americans to serve in the armed forces.

1861
The American Civil War begins, mainly because of slavery.

1919
The summer following World War I is marked by numerous race riots, especially in Chicago.

6

A TIMELINE

1950–1953
During the Korean War, the number of black troops fighting in the U.S. military increases substantially.

1968
The assassination of Dr. Martin Luther King Jr. brings new urgency to the civil rights movement.

1941–1945
After Japan bombs Hawai'i's Pearl Harbor on December 7, 1941, the United States enters World War II.

1941–1945   1948   1950–1953   1954–1975   1968   2001–2005

2001–2005
Former army general Colin Powell serves under President George W. Bush as the country's first African American secretary of state.

1948
President Harry S. Truman signs Executive Order 9981 on July 26, ending military segregation.

1954–1975
The Vietnam War integrates black and white troops, who are united in their belief that the war cannot be won.

INTRODUCTION

SECOND-CLASS CITIZENS

Ever since the African slave trade began in the 15th century, black people have often been treated as inferior to white people. A steady supply of unpaid workers quickly became integral to the American economy, especially in the South. White people regarded blacks as little more than cattle, property to be used however they saw fit. Slaves were bought and sold with no consideration of their personal circumstances, and they were often mistreated or abused without reservation or remorse by their owners. They were perceived as lesser beings in every way—from intelligence to inherent value. Even after slavery became illegal in the 19th century, these ideas of inequality persisted.

Denials and Rejections

The enduring and pervasive belief in white superiority meant that most requests for equality from the black community were flatly denied. For centuries, this included not being allowed to serve in the armed forces. During the American Revolution, whites feared letting black slaves serve because they would be using weapons that they could easily turn against their white owners. Later, objections were based on long-held beliefs that blacks did not have the physical abilities, mental discipline, or moral character required to carry out the variety of difficult tasks demanded of soldiers.

The military's refusal to permit blacks to join their ranks did not last for long. When it became clear that winning depended on having more soldiers, officers and administrators begrudgingly changed their stance, even if they still believed blacks were inferior. Because of this, black soldiers have participated in every American war.

Being allowed into the U.S. military did not translate to equal treatment,

LADIES' DEPARTMENT.

'Am I not a Woman and a Sister?'

White Lady, happy, proud and free,
Lend awhile thine ear to me ;
Let the Negro Mother's wail
Turn thy pale cheek still more pale.
Can the Negro Mother joy
Over this her captive boy,
Which in bondage and in tears,
For a life of wo she rears ?
Though she bears a Mother's name,
A Mother's rights she may not claim ;
For the white man's will can part,
Her darling from her bursting heart.

From the Genius of Universal Emancipation.
LETTERS ON SLAVERY.—No. III.

This poem is an example of one of the ways African Americans used writing to fight for equal rights.

Poet Paul Laurence Dunbar spoke out against the inequalities African Americans endured.

however. African Americans were typically issued the worst equipment and given lower quality uniforms than their white counterparts. As recently as World War II, black Americans were not allowed to be marines or air force pilots. They could join the navy—but only as workers in the mess hall, or cafeteria. The army allowed some black soldiers to fight, but only in all-black regiments that were usually led by white officers.

Free to Fight

In spite of the obstacles they faced, black Americans did join the military, willing to fight and die for their country. Ironically, many perished fighting for the very rights and liberties that neither they nor their children and grandchildren would get the chance to enjoy. Black poet Paul Laurence Dunbar noted in 1898 that the attitude of military leaders was essentially, "'Negroes, you may fight for us, but you may not vote for us. You may prove a strong bulwark [wall] when the bullets are flying, but you must stand from the line when the ballots are in the air.'"[1]

With little support or encouragement from the military or other soldiers, black soldiers fought on two fronts. They faced violence and danger from enemies on the battlefield, as well as from their white comrades in the barracks. Despite this abuse, many black soldiers exhibited courage, dignity, and astounding heroism while fighting for America.

CHAPTER ONE
LIBERTY FOR ALL?

George Washington made his opinion clear: No black person, free or enslaved, would be allowed to fight in the American Revolution. Like many southerners, Washington worried that giving blacks weapons would inevitably result in violent rebellions. However, it did not take long before he had little choice but to change his position. The number of soldiers engaged in the war was dropping drastically due to a combination of disease and desertion, and more were desperately needed if the patriots were to keep fighting. Reluctantly, white leaders gave permission for blacks to fight. Many of them made notable contributions to the American colonies' fight for independence from Britain in the 18th century.

Black men went on to fight in every major battle of the Revolution, from Lexington and Concord in Massachusetts to the decisive face-off at Yorktown in Virginia in 1781, where the colonists' victory led to an end to the war. Historians have noted that as many as 9,000 black men were enlisted as patriot soldiers and made up about 4 percent of the army.

A Chance for Freedom

For years before the war started, the topic of freedom and liberty from British rule was constantly discussed throughout the colonies. Both free and enslaved blacks were fascinated by the concept of a life of liberty. They hoped that if the colonists won their desired independence, it would naturally lead them to releasing blacks from their bondage.

Seven months before the first shots of the war were fired, representatives from each American colony met to decide how to respond to the growing threat of British aggression. This

This drawing from 1779 shows an African American artilleryman loading a cannon during the American Revolution.

group of representatives, known as the Continental Congress, decided that the colonies should create a network of militias to defend their towns and cities. To staff these militias, each colony would utilize a quarter of its available men. In addition, certain elite forces, called minutemen, would be established. Their name reflected the fact that these forces had to be capable of responding at a minute's notice, for no one knew when the first act of aggression would come.

Free blacks in the North were eager to join the militias as well as the minutemen forces. A few northern slaves also joined as assistants to their white masters. Southerners, by contrast, refused to allow blacks to serve. Allowing slaves to leave the plantations to serve in militias would cause economic hardship. Who would do all the work? Rebellions were another worry. In the south, the large number of slaves made uprisings a frightening possibility.

Battles and Losses

On April 19, 1775, 700 British troops began moving out of Boston, Massachusetts, suspicious that the colonists had a stockpile of weapons close to the nearby towns of Concord or Lexington. Boston resident Paul Revere and other patriots sounded the alarm, and when the British arrived in Lexington, they were met by armed minutemen. Shooting between the two forces lasted mere minutes. When the bullets stopped, eight minutemen were dead and nine were wounded. Only a single British soldier had been injured, however, so the British pushed on to Concord, where more than 300 patriots awaited them. This battle lasted longer, and after sustaining more substantial losses, the British fell back.

Although virtually no black soldiers were listed in the battle reports, historians know that some of the minutemen at Lexington and Concord were black. The name of Prince Estabrook, described only as "a Negro man," appears on a notice of casualties. Estabrook, a slave from Lexington, is the only name on the list that does not have "Mr." preceding it.

Soon after the battles at Lexington and Concord came the battle at Breed's Hill, often called the Battle of Bunker Hill. After this battle, two black militia soldiers received more than simply a passing notice from their commanding officers. Breed's Hill was the bloodiest battle of the entire war, as cannon fire pelted both armies. Participants later wrote that the hill, which overlooked Boston Harbor, was so slippery with blood that many of the men had difficulty keeping their balance.

This image depicts George Washington and other important figures in the American Revolution who were divided over whether to accept African American soldiers into their ranks.

A 25-year-old slave named Peter Salem, who had already fought at Concord, was one of 1,500 militia troops under the command of Colonel William Prescott at Breed's Hill. Salem and his fellow soldiers waited as British major John Pitcairn, who had commanded the forces at Lexington and Concord, led his assault. Concerned about their scant supply of ammunition, Prescott had warned his troops not to shoot until they were close enough to ensure they could inflict damage—or, as he put it, not "till you see the whites of their eyes."[2] When the British got within 50 yards (45.7 m) of the militia, Salem and the others opened fire, driving the British back. However, after a few moments, the militiamen were forced to retreat because their ammunition was almost gone. As Pitcairn jubilantly shouted that the British were once again victorious, Salem shot him.

An American militiaman wrote in his journal that "a Negro man belonging to Groton, took aim at Major Pitcairn, as he was rallying the dispersed British troops and shot him thro' the head."[3] Salem was singled out for his bravery and later rewarded.

A Controversial Order

The members of the Continental Congress closely followed the news of the early battles. Though they were pleased that the militias had done so well, it was clear that the recent clashes with the British were not isolated incidents. A full-scale war was inevitable, and local militias, no matter how brave, were no substitute for a real army. The Congress voted

This engraving shows the moment Major Pitcairn was shot by Peter Salem at the Battle of Bunker Hill.

to establish a Continental army made up of soldiers from all of the colonies. George Washington, a colonel from the Virginia militia, was chosen as the new army's commander-in-chief.

With the formation of the Continental army came some new dilemmas. Many of the congressional leaders were uneasy with the inclusion of any blacks—freemen or slaves. Some believed that even though blacks had performed admirably as minutemen, they might not be as brave or capable as white soldiers. A number also felt that the colonies should not allow slaves to serve in the army because their contribution would be, according to a committee from Massachusetts, "inconsistent with the principles that are to be supported, and reflect dishonor on this Colony."[4] In other words, it would be hypocritical to allow men who were not free to fight for the freedom of whites.

Washington remained against the idea of blacks in his army. After getting input from his war council as well as the Continental Congress, he finally issued a directive that "Neither Negroes, Boys unable to Bear Arms, nor old men unfit to endure the fatigues of the campaign, are to be enlisted."[5]

This directive immediately sparked protests, both from blacks already serving in militias and from a number of white officers. General John Thomas wrote a letter to John Adams, an important Massachusetts congressional delegate, insisting that to exclude black soldiers from the new army was a big mistake. "In the regiments at Roxbury," wrote Thomas, "we have some Negroes; but I look on them, in General, Equally Serviceable with other men ... many of them have proven themselves brave."[6]

A Need for Soldiers

Thomas's views on allowing blacks in the Continental army did not change the minds of the American military leaders, but Lord Dunmore, the royal governor of Virginia, took another approach. Loyal to the British cause, Dunmore issued a proclamation promising freedom to any slave who volunteered to fight with the British army.

Dunmore hoped that numerous slaves would immediately run to the British, thereby collapsing the entire southern economy and hurting the colonists' cause. He was accurate. Within three months of his proclamation, about 800 slaves had joined the British military. Dunmore's proclamation thus not only hurt the colonial economy but also convinced

"NO OTHER RECOMPENSE"

The slaves who joined the British army in hopes of attaining their freedom were often treated inhumanely. One of the most vivid examples occurred at Yorktown, the site of the final major battle of the war. As the British were under siege, supplies ran dangerously low, and rather than share food equally with everyone, officers cut the rations of the black soldiers. At first, those soldiers were given the spoiled biscuits and rotted meat that whites would not touch. When even that food ran out, the starving soldiers were driven away from the camp toward the American army.

Joseph Plumb, a young American who kept a diary during his years as a soldier, recalled his shock at seeing many black soldiers pushed away:

During the siege, we saw in the woods herds of Negroes which [the British general] Lord Cornwallis (after he inveigled [acquired] them from their proprietors), in love and pity to them, had turned adrift, with no other recompense for their confidence in his humanity than the smallpox for their bounty and starvation and death for their wages. They might be seen scattered about in every direction, dead and dying, with pieces of ears of burnt Indian corn in the hands and mouths, even of those that were dead.[1]

1. Quoted in Ray Raphael, *A People's History of the American Revolution: How Common People Shaped the Fight for Independence.* New York, NY: New Press, 2001, p. 269.

many blacks throughout the colonies that their only chance at freedom was a British victory.

Some slaves were so desperate to get away to the British that they fought their white owners. In Maryland, a Dorchester County court decided to deal severely with three slaves who had killed a white man in their rush to join Dunmore. To frighten other slaves and deter them from even thinking about escaping, the three men were sentenced to a grisly public execution.

In addition to Lord Dunmore's proclamation, Washington and his war council eventually decided to allow black soldiers to fight because they had a serious shortage of soldiers. Many soldiers' initial terms had expired, and they wanted to return home. Their farms—and their families—needed tending. There had been very little fighting after the first three battles of the war, and many of the American soldiers were restless. One Massachusetts soldier wrote to his wife, "Our People are all most Bewicht about getting home."[7]

Filling the ranks with more soldiers was crucial. Washington knew the fighting would escalate soon, so he advised the Continental Congress to order each colony to send more militias to replace departing soldiers. This time, black soldiers were allowed to enlist if they were freemen. Slaves were officially banned, but local recruitment boards had quotas to fill, and often looked the other way when slaves accompanied their masters into the army. Sometimes, too, a slave might be permitted to take the place of an owner who was not interested in fighting. As a result, many whites who had never owned a slave purchased one simply to use as their replacement in battle. Although white enlistees were given property or a monetary bonus in return for military service, many slaves were promised that they would be freed when the war ended.

Hard Times

No matter in what capacity a soldier served, life as a Continental soldier—black or white—was difficult. Food could be scarce, and the rations that did arrive at camp were often spoiled. The soldiers lacked boots, blankets, and warm uniforms. Often they went months without pay. Despite these hardships, and regardless of their color, the soldiers proved remarkably determined and resilient.

By the summer of 1776, there were black soldiers in almost every battalion of the Continental army. One soldier in the British army commented in his journal, "No regiment is to be seen in which there are not Negroes in abundance; and among them are able-bodied, strong, and brave fellows."[8] While some did fight on the battlefield, many of these black soldiers spent more time in support roles than in actual combat. They drove wagons, delivered supplies, dug graves, and sometimes worked as servants to officers.

Some, like James Armistead, were valuable spies. Armistead was assigned to the French general the Marquis de Lafayette, who accompanied a large French force sent to help the Americans in 1781. As part of his service, Armistead traveled back and forth between the American and

This certificate commends James Armistead for his service during the Revolution.

British encampments in Virginia. He was able to convince the British officers that he was spying for them, but he was actually a double agent gathering intelligence for the Americans.

Rhode Island's Solution

Separating soldiers based on their race was difficult and largely impractical, so the vast majority of black soldiers served in integrated units. However, a few all-black units received special attention during the Revolution. The most famous by far was the First Rhode Island Regiment, led by one of Washington's best young officers, Colonel Christopher Greene.

The regiment was created in 1778, following the loss of 2,500 soldiers to disease and lack of provisions after a long winter at Valley Forge, Pennsylvania. The state of Rhode Island was unable to recruit enough whites to meet its assigned quota, so its legislature made an attractive offer to its black population: "It is Voted and Resolved, that every able-bodied negro, mulatto, or Indian man-slave in the State may enlist ... to serve during the continuance of the present war ... [and] that every slave so enlisting shall, upon his passing muster by Col. Christopher Greene, be immediately discharged from the service of his master or mistress, and be absolutely free."[9]

The regiment was called into battle in August 1778, soon after its formation, to fight a mercenary army of German soldiers in the only battle waged in Rhode Island. Although the black troops ultimately lost the battle, they inflicted five times more casualties on the enemy than they received. In fact, the regiment put up such incredibly fierce resistance that the commander of the professional German army refused to make his men fight the next day—and asked for a transfer to another post.

One white veteran of the Battle of Rhode Island described the First Rhode Island's participation:

There was a black regiment in the same situation. Yes, a regiment of negroes, fighting for our liberty and independence—not a white man among them but the officers—stationed in the same dangerous and responsible position. Had they been unfaithful, or given way before the enemy, all would have been lost. Three times in succession were they attacked, with most desperate valor and fury, by well-disciplined and veteran troops, and three times did they successfully repel the assault, and thus preserve our army from capture. They fought through the war. They were brave, hardy troops.[10]

Reaping Rewards

Armies on both sides of the American Revolution praised the actions and bravery of black troops. Sadly, how these soldiers were treated once the war ended was often unfair or outright cruel. Some slaves were given their freedom as promised, including those in the First Rhode Island Regiment. Some of the slaves who had fought for the British were taken to places such as Nova Scotia and Jamaica and set free.

However, thousands who had dreamed of freedom never obtained

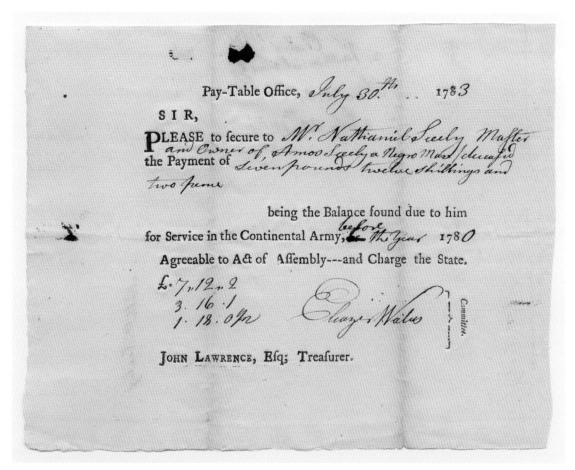

A slave owner submitted this form to the government requesting money to compensate him for the loss of his slave, who was killed fighting in the American Revolution.

it. The British transported many to the West Indies. There, blacks were sold to new owners or given as payment to British officers. Many black soldiers who had fought in place of their white American owners discovered that since they did not have a written guarantee for their freedom, they remained slaves. It was a tragic and bitter moment of irony that the people who had shed their blood and risked their lives in a war fought for freedom were denied that very reward.

CHAPTER TWO
A PERSONAL STAKE

Nearly 80 years after the American Revolution, the country again faced a deadly conflict, this one fought solely among its own people. As the American Civil War loomed on the horizon, African Americans were, once again, ready to enlist and fight for the rights of their embattled country. This time, African Americans had a very personal stake in the outcome of the national conflict. They wanted the North to win, and with that victory, they hoped to gain the freedom they had wanted for so long.

"Cease to Be Divided"

The American Civil War began largely over the institution of slavery. In the years since the Revolution, the northern states had abolished slavery, but it was still firmly entrenched in the South. There, slaves provided unpaid labor, and southern plantation owners recognized that the South's economy would collapse without it.

As the calls increased for slavery to be abolished nationally, tension grew between the North and South. The North argued slavery should be illegal everywhere. The South countered that each state should have the right to decide for itself. Of primary concern were the new states entering the Union, such as Kentucky and Missouri. Geographically, these states lay between the slave states of the South and the free Northern states.

Abraham Lincoln, who was elected president in 1860, had warned that the issue of slavery would tear the nation apart. "A house divided against itself cannot stand," he said in 1858. "I believe this government cannot endure, permanently half slave and half free. I do not expect the house to fall, but I do expect it will cease to be divided. It will become all one thing, or all the other."[11]

Confederate forces bombarded Fort Sumter in April 1861, setting off the Civil War.

His prediction was correct. Lincoln's election was a turning point for southern plantation owners, who believed their way of life was in danger, so South Carolina seceded, or declared itself separate, from the Union (the rest of the country). Six more states followed at that

time (more would join later), and the new Confederate States of America was formed in February 1861. Two months later, on April 12, 1861, South Carolina attacked Fort Sumter, a Union stronghold in South Carolina. Americans were officially at war with one another.

Menial Laborers

The North thought the war would last only a few months since the South, in theory, faced huge disadvantages. The North had 19 million whites, while the South had just over 8 million. The North also had multiple factories manufacturing weapons and war supplies, plus farms producing food. The South had very few of either—its economy was primarily built on cotton plantations.

Even though their chances of victory seemed small, southerners would not arm any of their 4 million slaves to fight for the new Confederacy. Most whites did not want to lose their free labor, and echoing the same fears from 1775, they worried that weapons in the hands of slaves would be turned against them. There was also still a widespread belief that blacks were incapable of being effective soldiers. In addition, a number of southerners agreed that it would send a mixed message to have blacks fighting alongside white slave owners. Clement H. Stevens, a Confederate general, said, "The justification of slavery in the South is the inferiority of the Negro. If we make him a soldier, we concede the whole question."[12]

The South did draft thousands of slaves into the war effort to perform menial labor. They helped with construction, cooked, dug latrines, and performed other general camp chores. This slave labor pool was so critical to the war effort, in fact, that historians have noted that it was set up even before the first white soldiers were drafted.

No Real Need

Black soldiers were no more welcome in the Union army than they were in the Confederate one. As soon as the war began, many black Americans flocked to enlist on behalf of the North. In New York, black leaders offered to raise the money to arm and assemble three black regiments. The black community in Philadelphia, Pennsylvania, offered to assemble two more, and in Washington, D.C., more than 100 men tried to enlist. Despite the South's insistence that the war was centered on the issue of states' rights, many of them believed the true cause of the war was slavery, and no one had a greater interest in the outcome of this bitter argument than black Americans.

The U.S. War Department turned down all of these offers. No one in the federal government thought that the war would last very long. Due to the South's apparent weaknesses, Lincoln and his aides put out a call for 75,000 white men to join the Union army for a 90-day term. They saw no need to expand the request to black soldiers.

Many African Americans were eager to serve in the Union army.

This decision provoked a great deal of criticism from the black community, especially from Frederick Douglass, the most influential black spokesman of that time. Douglass complained, "Colored men were good enough to fight under Washington, but they are not good enough to fight under [General George B.] McClellan." He predicted, "The side which first summons the Negro to its aid will conquer."[13]

Despite Douglass's prediction, many government officials believed that allowing black soldiers into the Union army was a mistake. Governor David Tod of Ohio felt that white soldiers would not wish to serve alongside blacks, and as a result, the unity of the army would suffer. "Do you know that this is a white man's government," he asked, "[and] that the white men are able to defend and protect it; and that to enlist a Negro soldier would be to drive every white man out of the service?"[14]

Rethinking Policies

The war proceeded without black soldiers on either side. Then, on July 21, 1861, just before the 90-day enlistments for Union soldiers ended, the Confederate army surprised the North by soundly defeating the Union army in a battle at Bull Run, Virginia. Lincoln realized he needed to increase the size of the Union army, so, against his personal opinions, he permitted 50,000 black men to join the army and serve in noncombat duties.

Many in the North believed that Lincoln was foolish for not taking advantage of the thousands of men who were willing to fight. John Andrew, the governor of Massachusetts, said that it seemed clear that the war was not going to be as short as originally predicted, and that the color of a man's skin should make no difference in wartime: "It is not my opinion that our generals, when any man comes to the standard and desires to defend the flag, will find it important to light a candle, and see what his complexion is, or to consult the family Bible to ascertain whether his grandfather came from the banks of the Thames or the banks of the Senegal."[15]

Douglass continued to pressure the government into rethinking its policy on black soldiers. He argued that the North would lose the war unless it could use all of its strength to fight the Confederacy—and that blacks

J. GAIL

Although black troops were allowed to join the military, they were usually given hard labor jobs such as building roads.

were a key part of that strength. "This is no time to fight with one hand, when both are needed," he said. "This is no time to fight only with your white hand, and allow your black hand to remain tied."[16]

Lincoln felt the pressure of public opinion, as well as pressure from his own generals, who were concerned by the disappointingly low number of soldiers enlisting by the fall of 1862. He already believed that slavery had to end in order to unite the country, and he recognized the practicality of admitting black soldiers to the fight. On New Year's Day, 1863, he issued the famous Emancipation Proclamation, which addressed both issues. The Emancipation Proclamation declared slaves in the Confederate states to be free, and also, for the first time, formally allowed African Americans to serve in the military.

"A Powerful Ally"

Now that the government's ban on black troops was over, the Union army rushed to create new black regiments, as well as to arm blacks who had previously been limited to supporting roles in the war. Douglass and other black leaders enthusiastically embraced the task of recruiting young men to join the all-black regiments. Douglass gave a stirring speech in March 1863, in which he shouted, "Men of color, to arms," and told his audience that "liberty won only by white men would lose half its luster."[17]

Ulysses S. Grant, commander of the Union army, was extremely pleased at the prospect of new soldiers. "By arming the Negro," he wrote to President Lincoln, "we have added a powerful ally. They will make good soldiers and taking them from the enemy weakens him in the same proportion they strengthen us."[18] Soon, black regiments were started in Iowa, Rhode Island, Connecticut, Pennsylvania, Illinois, Ohio, Michigan, and Indiana.

Of all the black regiments, the 1000-man 54th Infantry Regiment was the most famous. As the first one organized in the North after the Emancipation Proclamation, it captured the public's interest. After training and doing support work for other army regiments, the 54th finally got its chance to fight on July 18, 1863. Union army leaders wanted to take control over the Port of Charleston in South Carolina. However, to do that, they had to overpower Fort Wagner, which stood on an island at the entrance to the harbor.

The 54th charged at dusk, storming behind its color sergeant, the soldier who held the large American flag aloft. In those days, the flag of an army

REACTION TO A PROCLAMATION

In *American Patriots: The Story of Blacks in the Military from the Revolution to Desert Storm*, author Gail Buckley described the anticipation and reaction throughout the North as people heard for the first time that President Lincoln had issued the Emancipation Proclamation:

> *On New Year's Day, 1863, churches and meeting halls through-out the North were packed with people awaiting official con-firmation of Emancipation. When the news finally came on the [telegraph] wire, sometime after ten p.m., a one-hundred-voice choir broke into the "Hallelujah Chorus" at Boston's Tremont Temple, where Frederick Douglass [and other notables] were waiting, and where a human chain had been formed to the telegraph office. In Dracut, Massachusetts, Adrastus Lew, Underground Railroad conductor and Revolutionary descen-dant, and his wife were hosting an integrated party when the news was rushed in. They immediately formed a "Peace and Unity" club and decided to meet every year thereafter.*

> *On the fiftieth anniversary of the Proclamation, in 1913, [one black minister who witnessed the event] … recalled original Emancipation events in Washington. "Men squealed, women fainted, dogs barked, white and colored people shook hands, songs were sung and … cannons began to fire at the navy-yard, and follow in the wake of the roar that had for some time been going on behind the White House … It was indeed a time of times … nothing like it will ever be seen again in this life.*[1]

1. Gail Buckley, *American Patriots: The Story of Blacks in the Military from the Revolution to Desert Storm*. New York, NY: Random House, 2001, p. 88.

This is an illustration of Lincolns's first reading of the Emancipation Proclamation.

was such an important symbol that it was crucial that it never fall to the ground during a battle. Soon into the charge, the color sergeant was shot.

Another member of the 54th, a young sergeant named William Carney, hurried to take the flag. Armed with bayonets, the regiment was no match

for the cannons and huge naval guns of the fort. Lewis Douglass, the son of Frederick Douglass, was a soldier in the 54th. He recalled later that the bloodshed was horrific: "Men fell all around me," he said. "A shell would explode and clear a space of twenty feet, our men would close up again, but it was no use—we had to retreat, which was a very hazardous undertaking. How I got out of that fight alive, I cannot tell."[19]

Somehow, young Carney managed to keep the flag aloft. Though he was shot three times and severely wounded, he staggered into the medic's tent, uttering words that became famous throughout the Union army: "Boys, the old flag never touched the ground."[20] Because of the courage he displayed in that battle, Carney became the first black soldier ever to receive the Medal of Honor.

Almost half of the 54th Infantry was killed, wounded, or captured during that battle, but by then, the regiment had made a name for itself. Now, no one doubted that black soldiers could fight.

Poor Treatment

While the Union claimed to be pleased with how black soldiers conducted themselves on the battlefield, the army's treatment of those soldiers told a different story. No matter how well trained and competent black soldiers were, they were promoted less frequently than white soldiers and almost never reached the same ranks as their white compatriots. Even after black regiments displayed bravery and heroism, they still spent the majority of their time doing backbreaking labor that white troops were rarely asked to do.

Perhaps the most glaring difference, however, was in the wages that black and white soldiers were paid. The lowest-ranking white soldier received $13 per month plus a clothing allowance of $3.50. Black soldiers received $10 with a $3 clothing allowance deducted from that wage. White soldiers were given pay raises for time served and promotions. Black soldiers—no matter how long and well they served, or at what rank—never received any raises.

Black soldiers, many of their white officers, and others who had called for black inclusion into the army were outraged. Eventually, under pressure from Lincoln and state leaders, Congress finally enacted legislation in 1864 that guaranteed equal pay for black and white troops.

Remembering Fort Pillow

In addition to inequities in pay and promotions, black soldiers faced more deadly problems. Soon after the North began allowing black regiments to fight, the Confederacy announced that any black Union soldiers captured in battle would not be treated as regular prisoners of war. Instead, they would be considered either runaway slaves (even though many were freemen) or insurgents. As punishment, they would be shot. In addition, the Confederate congress passed a law stating that all captured white officers of black regiments could be executed.

Lincoln responded in kind, stating that for every white Union officer or black soldier killed while a captive of the Confederacy, a Confederate prisoner would be shot. Nonetheless, Confederate soldiers committed many atrocities on battlefields during the war, often killing black soldiers who tried to surrender rather than taking them prisoner. One of the most infamous examples is the

During the attack on Fort Wagner in Charleston in 1863, the all-black 54th regiment played an important role.

SAILING TO FREEDOM

One of the most famous black heroes of the Civil War was a South Carolina seaman named Robert Smalls. Although he was a slave, he was also an expert navigator, having been sailing ships since he was a child. On the Confederate ship *Planter*, he worked as a pilot, but he was labeled a wheelman since he could not outrank white sailors. Smalls was ambitious; he had no intention of remaining a slave and planned to make his escape quickly.

Late on the night of March 13, 1862, when the docked *Planter* was loaded with weapons to be delivered to a nearby fort and the captain and other white officers were sleeping in Charleston, Smalls quietly smuggled his wife and young children aboard. With the Confederate flag flying from the mast, Smalls put on the overcoat and hat worn by the captain and set out to sea. When he safely passed the other Confederate ships guarding the harbor from Northern ships, he put up a white flag of truce and turned his ship over to a Union vessel anchored just outside the blockade.

Union soldiers took Smalls to meet President Lincoln, who thanked him for his bravery. Smalls then became a captain in the Union navy, and after the war, he was elected to the U.S. Congress. An impressive speaker, he engaged in many congressional debates about equal rights. The "negro was here to stay, and it was to the interests of the white man to see that he got all of his rights," he once said. A bust of Smalls stands at the Tabernacle Baptist Church in Beaufort, South Carolina. A plaque below it states, "My race needs no special defense, for the past history of them in this country proves them to be the equal of any people anywhere. All they need is an equal chance in the battle of life."[1]

1. Quoted in Douglas Egerton, "Terrorized African-Americans Found their Champion in Civil War Hero Robert Smalls," *Smithsonian*, September 2018. www.smithsonianmag.com/history/ terrorized-african-americans-champion-civil-war-hero-robert-smalls-180970031/.

massacre carried out in April 1864 against soldiers at the Union's Fort Pillow in Tennessee. Led by General Nathan Bedford Forrest, more than 1,500 Confederate troops stormed the fort, which was manned by about 550 Union soldiers, many of whom were black. Black soldiers who tried to surrender were savagely butchered, and the final death toll was high. Widely condemned throughout the North, the Fort Pillow massacre inspired black troops to later use "Remember Fort Pillow!" as a rallying cry.

Most black soldiers did not experience violence as extreme as that at Fort Pillow, although they were treated poorly in countless other ways by the armies on both sides. Despite the obstacles they faced, many succeeded admirably—and often heroically—on the battlefield. By the end of the war, 198,000 black soldiers had served in the Union army and navy. They had participated in 449 engagements with the enemy, 39 of which were major battles. Just less than one-third of them died during the war. There was no doubt that black soldiers had made the ultimate sacrifice.

Once the Civil War was over, African American soldiers were understandably proud of the role they had played in ending slavery and securing freedom for all black Americans. As they had hoped, liberty was now officially the law of the land. The future seemed bright for these soldiers and their families, who, after making significant sacrifices, now envisioned lives characterized by equality and fairness. Tragically, reality proved substantially different.

CHAPTER THREE
THE WORLD
AT WAR

In less than a century, the young United States had weathered two major conflicts, the American Revolution and the Civil War. Men had died on all sides in the battles for freedom. In the years after the Civil War, the weary nation chose peace, but the government knew that new threats or conflicts—from within or without—might be just over the horizon. The federal government believed there was still a need for armed forces and decided to maintain an army of 56,000 men. This time around, blacks were permitted to serve with far fewer restrictions on what roles they could assume. In these postwar years, one in five soldiers was African American. They served in one of four active black units.

On the Frontier

Once the Civil War was over, people began looking beyond their boundaries and joining the movement to settle the West. Every day, more Americans were packing their belongings, loading wagons, and hitching up horses to head west. Some went in the hopes of becoming permanent settlers, while others were workers laying railroad track or erecting telegraph lines. Soldiers stationed west of the Mississippi River were given the job of protecting those coming to these unknown and sometimes dangerous lands. Often, settlers were threatened by Native Americans, who fought back against whites taking their land.

For understandable reasons, there was a great deal of hostility between U.S. soldiers and Native American tribes. The soldiers were there to take control of tribal lands and claim them for the United States, regardless of the cost and hardship to Native Americans. Often this was done with violence and cruelty, with Native

Many African Americans worked on building railroads, a priority in the late 1800s to help people travel faster and easier.

Americans imprisoned, forcibly moved, or killed. Despite such treatment, some of the Native Americans actually respected the black cavalrymen. They considered them brave and tenacious fighters, calling them "buffalo soldiers" because the men's dark skin and coarse hair reminded them of the buffalo. Over time, the term came to be used for all black cavalry troops.

The buffalo soldiers received respect from the Native Americans but not from their own army officials. They were almost always given the most dangerous assignments and issued the worst equipment and uniforms. To help deal with inadequate uniforms and cold temperatures, some of the black soldiers wore coats made from buffalo fur, further reflecting their nickname.

Praise and Prejudice

Though they were not treated well, buffalo soldiers did earn praise from fellow soldiers and white officers who observed their performance in combat. When four regiments of buffalo soldiers were sent to Cuba to fight in the Spanish-American War in 1898, a white officer admitted that he was amazed at their ability to fight. "I must say," he said, "that I never saw braver men anywhere."[21]

Members of the 25th infantry, some wearing the buffalo coats that helped earn them the nickname of buffalo soldiers, pose for a photo taken in Montana.

Such praise was worth nothing back home, however. As buffalo soldiers returned from their tours of duty—either from the western frontier or from the war in Cuba—it was clear that the emancipation and freedom Lincoln had promised African Americans had not materialized.

Racial discrimination was everywhere, and it was especially bad in the South, where states had enacted "Jim Crow" laws that restricted the rights and privileges of African Americans. These laws made it illegal for black people to use the same public water fountains or restrooms as white people and dictated what schools their children could attend and in which neighborhoods they could buy a home. No matter how heroically a black soldier had fought for the United States, he was viewed with distrust or even outright hatred in the South. There were countless incidents of returning African

EXPLORING THE LEGACY

In the National Museum of African American History and Culture, part of the Smithsonian in Washington, D.C., there is a display honoring buffalo soldiers. The display features artifacts, including photographs, uniforms, medals, and examples of buffalo robes made by the Native Americans and often worn by the soldiers for warmth.

In Houston, Texas, an entire museum is dedicated to the legacy of buffalo soldiers. Exhibits cover their roles in the various wars the United States has fought from 1770 to 2000, and an artillery section features the weaponry and munitions used by the buffalo soldiers, including rifles, muskets, and cannonballs.

American soldiers in uniform being thrown out of restaurants or bars, refused service in stores, and denied seats on streetcars.

Historians say that the discrimination in the South was worse for black soldiers than for black civilians. Since the American Revolution, the idea of an armed black man had terrified many southerners. To them, black troops were frightening and offensive.

African Americans returning from the war in Cuba were especially at risk when their trains passed through southern cities. One train carrying young African American soldiers stopped in the middle of the night in Nashville, Tennessee. As the soldiers slept, 200 civilians and 75 police officers armed with guns and clubs boarded the train and attacked them. Other black soldiers recalled being spit at, called names, and threatened as they walked down the street in their uniforms.

Bearing the Burden

In 1917, President Woodrow Wilson declared that the United States was entering World War I in order to help the Allies (including France and England) defeat Germany and other nations that made up the Central Powers. Considering the mistreatment black Americans endured, it is not surprising that many were reluctant to participate. The black newspaper the *Messenger* published an editorial urging black men not to enlist: "We are conscripting the Negro into the military and industrial establishments to achieve this end for white democracy four thousand miles away,

while the Negro at home, though bearing the burden in every way, is denied economic, political, educational, and civil democracy."[22]

On the other hand, black leaders and writers such as W.E.B. Du Bois believed the war could provide an opportunity for African Americans to lead the struggle for equality at home while fighting for democracy in Europe. He urged them, "while the war lasts, to forget our special grievances and close our ranks shoulder to shoulder with our own white fellow citizens and the allied nations that are fighting for democracy."[23]

In the end, hundreds of thousands of African American soldiers did enlist, but it soon became clear that discrimination against black soldiers had only gotten worse. Though the U.S. Army relied on black soldiers to provide the manpower it needed, it was unwilling to support them or treat them with respect.

Out in the Cold

Once again, black troops were poorly equipped compared to their white counterparts. For example, in army camps where soldiers trained before shipping out, white soldiers received new uniforms, while the black officers were often forgotten. Sometimes African American troops even got old Civil War uniforms, much to the amusement of the white soldiers. "When one of the organizations thus clad marched through the camp," one historian wrote, "it became the laughingstock of the rest of the soldiers, and the men were humiliated."[24]

More serious were the living quarters provided at U.S. camps. Black troops were not permitted to sleep in sturdy barracks, but instead were given tents without stoves for heat. This proved disastrous for many young black recruits at Camp Alexander, Virginia. During the winter of 1917, the lack of warm clothes, blankets, and stoves resulted in a large number of deaths. In a 1918 report to the secretary of war, an officer reported that during that winter, "men died like sheep in their tents, it being a common occurrence to go around in the morning and drag men out frozen to death."[25]

The assignments the men received proved to be one of the biggest disappointments of all. Many blacks had enlisted to fight, but instead of being slated for combat duty, they were once again expected to perform menial labor—building roads, cooking, cleaning, and driving supply trucks. These jobs would not help them advance or prove themselves as valuable assets in the war effort. In fact, of the 200,000 African American troops sent to France, only 40,000 saw any combat.

A Welcome from the French

The black combat units who were sent to France presented a problem for U.S. military leaders. Brigadier General Lytle Brown, the director of war planning, was not convinced that blacks would conduct themselves well in battle. In addition, since integrating the army was not even a consideration, he also worried about the problem of how to keep white and black troops separate in the field.

To sidestep the issue, the U.S. military decided to loan large contingents of African American troops to the French, who had lost more than 200,000 soldiers since the war's beginning in 1914. French commanders, desperate for replacements, were overjoyed to add the black soldiers to their ranks. Since the French did not have a history of racial discrimination, the black Americans were more than willing to join their units.

It soon became clear that the French and African American soldiers were a good match. Ironically, this worried the American military leaders. They noticed that the French treated the black soldiers as equals—a

The French army welcomed the bravery and skill shown by black troops.

development that they felt would be a great problem when the troops eventually returned home. The African Americans would almost certainly want to be treated the same way in the United States, and, just as certainly, white Americans—especially those in the South— would never do that.

In order to educate the French on how "best" to treat African Americans, U.S. leaders created a document, entitled "Secret Information Concerning Black American Troops." The document explained, "Although a citizen of the United States, the black man is regarded by the white American as an inferior being with whom relations of business or service only are possible." The black man, it said, has vices which "are a constant menace to the American who has to repress them sternly." The document warned the French not to be too familiar or friendly with blacks: "We may be courteous and amiable ... but we cannot deal with them on the same plane as with white American officers ... We must not eat with them, must not shake hands or seek to talk or meet with them outside the requirements of military service."[26]

The French government denounced the document. It promptly passed a resolution in the National Assembly to condemn such prejudice and affirm the equality of all, no matter what class, religion, or race. The French military was impressed with the bravery and courage shown by the African American troops—and they witnessed their heroism almost immediately on the battlefield.

From Harlem to the Trenches

The first group of African American troops to report to the front were members of the 369th Infantry Regiment; most of them came from the Harlem section of New York City. The 369th soon experienced the horrors of trench warfare, in which the German and French armies traded artillery and machine-gun fire from their trenches. These were often

A helmet worn by members of the 369th is on display at the Smithsonian's National Museum of African American History and Culture in Washington, D.C.

THE PRINTED WEAPON

In addition to guns and tanks, Germany used propaganda as a weapon in World War I, distributing leaflets that attempted to take advantage of the discriminatory treatment African Americans received in the United States and make them less willing to risk their lives fighting for their country. The following is an example:

Do you enjoy the same rights as the white people do in America, the land of Freedom and Democracy? Or aren't you rather treated over there as second class citizens? ... Why then fight the Germans only for the benefit of the Wall-street robbers to protect the millions they have lent to the English, French and Italians? You have been made the tool of the egotistic and rapacious rich in England and in America, and there is nothing in the whole game for you but broken bones, horrible wounds, spoiled health, or death ... Let those do the fighting who make profit out of this war; don't allow them to use you as cannon food. To carry the gun in this war is not an honor but a shame. Throw it away and come over to the German lines. You will find friends who help you along.[1]

1. "To the colored soldiers of the U.S. Army," History Matters, accessed on April 6, 2019. historymatters.gmu.edu/d/6655/.

no more than 40 to 50 yards (37 to 46 m) apart, with barbed wire strung along the length of the trenches for protection.

It was in this setting that two members of the 369th showed their courage. Privates Henry Johnson and Needham Roberts were on sentry duty one night soon after arriving in France. They were on guard between the two trenches, making sure no German soldiers tried to cross through the barbed wire to kill Allied soldiers.

When Johnson and Roberts heard the sound of wire clippers,

they shouted a warning to their fellow soldiers back in the trenches and began throwing grenades at the patrol of 24 German soldiers. Both men were wounded but continued to fight. Roberts threw grenades at the raiding party, while Johnson struck several soldiers with the butt of his rifle. As two Germans tried to take Roberts prisoner, Johnson attacked them with a knife. The frightened Germans retreated, and the Allied soldiers—except for Roberts and Johnson—escaped unhurt.

Because of their heroic efforts to keep their fellow soldiers safe from the German raiders, Johnson and Roberts received one of the highest military honors bestowed in the French army—the Croix de Guerre (Cross of War). The 369th soon became famous for the actions of its brave, tireless soldiers. The regiment remained at the front for 191 consecutive days—a length of time almost unheard of during World War I. While Johnson and Roberts were the first to win French war medals, they were not the only members of the 369th who did. More than 100 men in that regiment were awarded the Croix de Guerre or the even more prestigious Medaille Militaire (military medal). Their fierceness earned African American infantrymen of the 369th the nickname "Hellfighters" from the German soldiers, who came to fear them.

Flying for the French

Another African American who won French medals was a pilot named Eugene Jacques Bullard. Born in Georgia, Bullard saved enough money to take a ship to France—a place his father had said was far more civil to black people than the United States. In 1917, Bullard joined the French Flying Corps and got his pilot's license, an opportunity he would not have had in the United States. No African Americans were permitted to enlist in the U.S. Air Corps, as the air force was called then, or the Marine Corps.

Bullard was a skilled pilot and quickly earned the respect of his fellow French pilots. He was nicknamed the "Black Swallow of Death" because of his ability to bring down German planes.

Other Americans also flew for France. They had come over in 1914, three years before the United States officially entered the war. When the United States joined the war in 1917, the U.S. Air Corps invited all American pilots already flying for France to now switch to the U.S. force. Bullard requested to join but was denied because he was black.

Bullard said after the war that while

the Americans had rejected him, he knew that people everywhere were interested in his career. "I was determined to do all that was in my power to make good," he said, "as I knew the eyes of the world were watching me as the first Negro military pilot in the world."[27] As he became one of the best fighter pilots in the French Flying Corps, he demonstrated that America's loss was France's gain.

"A Frenzy of Pride and Joy and Love"

On November 11, 1918, World War I ended with victory by the Allies. The French commander expressed appreciation to the African American troops who had fought with the French. One French general, who had commanded the famous Red Hand Division, pledged that he and his men would always remember the 371st and 372nd black regiments who had been attached to his division. "Dear friends from America," he said, "when you have recrossed the ocean, do not forget the Red Hand Division. Our pure brotherhood in arms has been consecrated in the blood of the brave. These bonds will never be severed."[28]

Fewer appreciative words for the black soldiers came from the United States. Though there were large parades in Paris to celebrate the Allied victory, American generals did not allow black troops to participate. In addition, many African American troops were ordered to stay in Europe to gather and bury the remains of the dead, rebuild bridges and roads, and even load coal onto the warships that took white troops back to the United States.

One exception was the 369th, which was the first New York regiment to return home. Its troops marched up Fifth Avenue and eventually into Harlem as huge crowds lined the streets. "A quarter of a million of men, women, and children of the colored race went wild with a frenzy of pride and joy and love," wrote one participant later. "For the final mile or so of our parade, about every fourth soldier of the ranks had a girl upon his arm—and we marched through Harlem singing and laughing."[29]

An Unsafe Country

Despite the welcoming response to the 369th, African American troops quickly learned that their efforts in yet another war had done nothing to improve their status in the United States. Obtaining civil rights in their own country was a bigger battle than the war against Germany had been. President Woodrow Wilson proclaimed that "the world must be made safe for democracy" in 1917.

The Harlem Hellfighters had their own jazz band, shown here in New York after returning from World War I.

However, this seemed to apply only to a portion of America's population. A. Philip Randolph, the editor of the *Messenger*, responded by writing, "We would rather make Georgia safe for the Negro."[30]

Instead of being grateful to African American soldiers for the sacrifices and dangers they had faced during the war, whites, especially in the South, felt like these returning men needed to be "taught a lesson." The French had treated blacks as equals; now it was the duty of Americans to teach these veterans that this was a mistake. Returning soldiers were attacked. Some were even killed by lynch mobs while the victims were still in uniform.

W.E.B. Du Bois wrote a passionate editorial in May 1919, saying, "It was right for us to fight. The faults of our country are our faults. Under similar circumstances, we would fight again. But by the God of Heaven, we are cowards and [fools] if now that that war is over, we do not marshal every ounce of our brain and brawn to fight a sterner, longer, more unbending battle against the forces of hell in our own land."[31]

In contrast, in a 1918 speech in New Orleans, one white Louisiana official summed up the South's position on returning black soldiers: "You ... are wondering how you are going to be treated after the war. Well, I'll tell you, you are going to be treated exactly like you were before the war; this is a white man's country and we expect to rule it."[32]

The attacks, the lynchings, and the ongoing disrespect and injustice from white America was more than demoralizing for the country's black veterans. It felt like an outright betrayal. As one black newspaper, the *Hot Springs Echo*, wrote sarcastically, "For valor displayed in the recent war, it seems that the Negro's particular decoration is to be the 'double-cross.'"[33]

CHAPTER FOUR
WORKING FOR A DOUBLE VICTORY

It quickly became obvious that life in the United States was far from being what many blacks had hoped for. The hate group called the Ku Klux Klan was growing increasingly powerful, and Jim Crow laws throughout the South were more entrenched than ever. In what became known as the Great Migration, thousands of blacks living in the South moved to the North, where equality—or at least better treatment—was more likely. After fighting overseas and proving themselves, it was easier for many black veterans to stand up for their civil rights.

By the late 1930s, as another war loomed on the horizon, more than a million black Americans lined up to enlist, even in the face of the ongoing attitude that African American soldiers were less competent than white soldiers. Their participation in World War II would be considered a watershed moment in racial history. Desegregation was still a dream, but the events of World War II laid the foundation for the civil rights movement of the 1950s and 1960s.

The Red Summer

After World War I, when whites continued to abuse black citizens as they had in years past, blacks—including veterans—felt more empowered to fight back. For six months, beginning in the spring of 1919, there were 26 race riots throughout the United States. Some of the worst clashes occurred in Chicago, Illinois, spurred by an event on July 27. A group of black teens floating on a raft in the lake drifted over the invisible line that marked the black and white sides of the beach. A white man got angry and began throwing rocks at the kids. One 17-year-old boy, Eugene Williams, fell off the raft and

Stonings were part of the awful violence during the Red Summer riots.

drowned. When police officers refused to arrest the man who had started the fight, the black community exploded in anger. Soon, 38 people were dead, and more than 500 were injured. Because of the rioting in Chicago and other cities around the country, this period became known as the "Red Summer," a reference to all the bloodshed.

Society's discrimination and inequality were mirrored in the military. Although African American leaders had made repeated requests for integration, as well as for more efficient use of black troops, there had been almost no reforms in the armed services. Neither the marines nor the air corps allowed blacks to join. In the navy, blacks were usually relegated to doing menial kitchen work in the mess or were assigned to laundry detail. The army primarily used black enlistees as laborers, and most leaders never acknowledged black contributions of any kind.

Campaign Promises

By the end of the 1930s, the United States, watching Europe edge closer and closer to another war, was building up its military forces again. In the past, African Americans had been largely ignored until the nation went to war and needed the manpower. This time, black leaders wanted President Franklin D. Roosevelt to ensure that blacks would have more opportunities in the military. They wanted

A LONG, DARK SHADOW

In February 2019, for the 100th anniversary of the Red Summer, the Grace Chorale of Brooklyn, New York, performed a concert, titled "A Long Dark Shadow," to commemorate those dark days. "Most Americans aren't that familiar with that summer," said Jason Asbury, the choir's director, "but many historians argue that it was one of the most troubling events of American history … The more I learned about the Red Summer, the more I saw that the foundation of the civil rights movement and the events of the 1960s were mobilized in 1919."[1]

One song featured in the program was called "A Stone to the Head: The Death of Eugene Williams." The song, written by two Princeton University music graduates, tells the story of the ill-fated trip on the lake. A number of people in the choir had trouble singing the song. "The first rehearsal we went through the score, I think everyone was uncomfortable reading this text about a white mob lynching an African American," said Asbury. He added, "There's no escaping the legacy of how this country has treated African Americans in the last 400 years, and it's up to us to untangle that and to address that legacy as individuals."[2]

1. Quoted in Kevin Duggan, "Cry of the Century: Brooklyn Heights Choir Recalled the 'Red Summer' of 1919," *Brooklyn Paper*, February 26, 2019. www.brooklynpaper.com/stories/42/9/24-red-summer-grace-chorale-2019-03-01-bk.html.

2. Quoted in Duggan, "Cry of the Century."

African American troops to be used as combat soldiers, fighter pilots, technical support personnel, and artillery gunners—not just relegated to menial labor.

Roosevelt, who had taken office in 1933, had claimed during his campaigns to support black equality. In 1940, when running for a third term, Roosevelt knew he needed African American voter support, so he made some concessions to black civil rights leaders who were demanding changes in the military. He added black advisors to the War Department and promoted Colonel Benjamin O. Davis, a veteran of the Spanish-American War, to brigadier general—the first African American ever to achieve that rank. He also assured black leaders that he

Brigadier General Benjamin O. Davis represented the black troops' hopes that equality was finally within reach.

supported equal opportunity for black troops in all branches of the military and promised to do something about the injustice.

The promotion of Davis and the addition of blacks to the War Department were welcome but long overdue. Civil rights leaders saw Roosevelt's actions as little more than symbolic gestures rather than part of a real commitment. They were not at all confident that Roosevelt's promises for sweeping change would become reality.

Although black leaders kept pressing Roosevelt to end military segregation, the president had little success convincing War Department generals that it was a good idea. They insisted that having black and white soldiers living together in barracks or on warships or serving in the same army units would prove disastrous. Some said that white troops would never stand for it. Morale would plummet. A spokesman for the generals reminded black leaders that segregation was not the military's fault, nor was it the military's responsibility to fix it.

The African American community was unwilling to accept this excuse, and Roosevelt knew that if blacks did not enlist because of unfair racial policies in the military, it would certainly hurt the war effort. He began to pressure military leaders in the various branches to rethink their position about including and effectively using black troops.

An Overlooked Hero

War had been raging in other parts of the world since 1939, but, on December 7, 1941, the Japanese attacked U.S. ships at Pearl Harbor, Hawai'i. Roosevelt immediately declared war on Japan, and the United States entered World War II on the side of the Allies, the largest of which were Great Britain, France, and Russia. Ironically, the first hero of this new war was a shy, 22-year-old black mess attendant in the U.S. Navy who was serving on the USS *West Virginia*, one of the ships at Pearl Harbor.

Like almost all other African Americans in the navy, Dorie Miller spent most of his day doing menial work such as cleaning, gathering dirty laundry, and helping to prepare and serve meals. When the bombs from the warplanes hit his ship, he raced to the captain, who had been severely wounded, and moved him to a more protected area. Although Miller had never been trained to use any weapons on the ship, he grabbed a .50 caliber antiaircraft gun when the man firing it was wounded and began shooting at the incoming planes. Miller brought down at least two Japanese warplanes, although witnesses said

IN PURSUIT

At the onset of World War II, Congress had finally passed laws allowing African Americans more opportunities with the armed services. However, the military continued to procrastinate, especially when asked to train blacks as fighter pilots. As always, people worried that having black and white troops training in the same facility would cause problems. Finally, thanks in large part to First Lady Eleanor Roosevelt, who had often championed the rights of blacks, the War Department relented. In 1941, it established a separate school for black airmen at the Tuskegee Army Airfield in Alabama.

The school began with a class of 13 student pilots. After seven months of grueling classroom and air training, the first cadets, including Benjamin O. Davis Jr., the son of America's only black general, completed the program. The men were known as the 99th Pursuit Squadron, but they called themselves the Lonely Eagles because they remained separate from the rest of the air corps.

Although many white pilots were convinced that the African American airmen would not be able to perform well in battle, they were highly successful during the 1944 invasion of Italy. In fact, the 99th Pursuit Squadron accounted for the highest number of German planes shot out of the sky. Led by Davis, the growing number of Tuskegee-trained airmen flew more than 15,000 missions.

The graduating classes from the Tuskegee Army Airfield brought their expertise to the aerial battles of World War II.

that he actually hit four. "It wasn't hard," Miller said later. "I just pulled the trigger and she worked fine. I had watched the others with these guns. I guess I fired her for about fifteen minutes."[34]

In all, 106 men on the *West Virginia* were killed and 52 were wounded, but experts said Miller's actions prevented an even greater loss of life. However, there was little mention of Dorie Miller from the navy after this battle. When asked to describe the events on the *West Virginia* that day, navy officials brushed off Miller as an unimportant worker and did not even give his name.

When Miller's name was finally released three months later, black newspapers around the country campaigned for him to receive the Medal of Honor. The secretary of the navy and other military leaders refused. Finally, on May 27, 1942, Miller received the recognition he was due when the navy awarded him the Navy Cross—the first African American ever to receive that medal.

The Double-V

When the United States declared war after the Pearl Harbor attack, African Americans turned out to enlist. This time, there was a different mood within the black community. This war would be waged not only on international battlefields, but also at home, as black citizens fought for an end to segregation and the hated Jim Crow laws. Blacks referred to the struggle as the Double-V, named after the V formed by the index and second finger, used by Allied leaders as a symbol of victory. James G. Thompson, a black cafeteria worker from Kansas, explained the Double-V in a 1942 letter to the *Pittsburgh Courier*:

The V for victory sign is being displayed prominently in all so-called democratic countries ... then let we colored Americans adopt the double VV for a double victory. The first V for victory over our enemies from without, the second V for victory over our enemies from within. For surely those who perpetuate these ugly prejudices here are seeking to destroy our democratic form of government just as surely as the Axis forces [of Germany, Japan, and Italy].[35]

Dashed Hopes

Any hope that the military had abandoned its policies of segregation and discrimination soon evaporated for African American soldiers. Every barracks, dining facility, and meeting room was organized with the idea of keeping black and white soldiers separate. On many southern bases, buses that were supposed to shuttle soldiers back and forth to town would not allow blacks to ride. Even chapels operated under the Jim Crow laws. On most military bases they listed schedules for four services: Catholic, Jewish, Protestant, and Negroes.

Many black soldiers were furious that German prisoners of war brought back to the United States were frequently given better treatment than they were. One officer said that he and other African American soldiers at his military base had to sit in the last two rows of the base movie theater, while prisoners of war sat in front with the white Americans. At Camp Barkeley, Texas, another black soldier was appalled to observe "a sign in the latrine, actually segregating a section of the latrine for Negro soldiers, the other being used by the German prisoners and the white soldiers."[36]

One of the oddest forms of segregation involved the blood supplies in military hospitals. In 1941, the Red Cross, pressured by army and navy leaders, announced that its blood banks would no longer accept blood plasma donated by blacks. According to Red Cross officials, white soldiers were refusing plasma if they knew it came from blacks. The decision was especially ironic since a black man, Dr. Charles Drew, had pioneered the collection and storage of blood for transfusions.

Underused and Unappreciated

Faced with consistent discrimination in the military, African American leaders and the black press stepped up pressure on the Roosevelts to keep their promises. Although the armed forces had made concessions in allowing blacks to enlist, military leaders consistently kept the new recruits in the same types of menial jobs they had held before. One black man who had a degree in biochemistry was allowed into the air force, much to his satisfaction. He did well in his training and hoped to be sent overseas. Instead, he was sent to another military camp, where he was made a laborer. "It is a mockery," he angrily wrote to his wife, "let no one tell you differently, this sudden opening of the so-called exclusive branches of the services to Negroes. We are trained, become skilled—and then the oblivion of common labor."[37]

The underutilization of blacks in World War II was felt not only by men, but also by black women who had joined the newly formed Women's Army Corps, or WAC. The WAC enlistees' purpose was to support American troops as secretaries, stenographers, telephone operators, and even ambulance drivers. Black WACs, however, were disappointed to learn that instead of providing such services, they mopped, swept, and scrubbed—sometimes even for white WACs. At Fort Jackson, South Carolina, for example, black WACs who had extensive training as medical technicians were put to work washing walls and doing other menial tasks. Such assignments frequently created an atmosphere of resentment and discouragement within the ranks.

An Exceptional Unit

Occasionally, however, there were exceptions. Some African American troops reached the front lines of battle and achieved remarkable successes. The 761st Tank Battalion, or Black Panthers, was one. The battalion was formed after Roosevelt pressured the War Department to set up a few black artillery units, even though white military leaders had long maintained that black troops lacked the ability to master large artillery weapons.

Throughout most of the war, the 761st saw no action. Its members trained in the United States and experienced the typical racism and discrimination. When they traveled by troop train to Fort Knox,

During the war, many African American WACs spent time sorting mail, even though they were often trained for more skilled work.

DANGEROUS DUTY

One of the most infamous incidents involving African American troops during World War II occurred at Port Chicago on Mare Island, California. On July 17, 1944, a large ammunition depot exploded, and more than 200 black sailors were killed. There was no greater loss of life on continental U.S. soil during the war, and that one explosion accounted for more than 15 percent of casualties of naval personnel.

The fact that the sailors who died were black, and thus had been given no other choice but to be laborers, enraged the black civilian community, who had been critical of the limited role of blacks in the war. When operations at the port resumed several days after the explosion, 258 African American sailors refused to work, stating that they felt that they lacked training and safety measures for such dangerous duty.

Most of the sailors, however, were eventually pressured into returning to their labor jobs at Port Chicago. Fifty who did not return were court-martialed, sentenced to hard labor for 8 to 15 years, and given dishonorable discharges. After the war, their convictions were overturned. Their attorney, Thurgood Marshall, who would later become a Supreme Court justice, declared, "This is not fifty men on trial for mutiny. This is the Navy on trial for its whole vicious policy toward Negroes ... Negroes in the Navy don't mind loading ammunition. They just want to know why they are the only ones doing the loading!"[1]

1. Quoted in Gail Buckley, *American Patriots: The Story of Blacks in the Military from the Revolution to Desert Storm*. New York, NY: Random House, 2001, p. 310.

Kentucky, they were told to keep the shades drawn because some white Kentuckians liked to shoot at trains carrying black soldiers.

In October 1944, the battalion finally got the chance to see combat. General George Patton's Third Army was pinned down by the Germans in France and needed artillery support. Because other artillery was assigned elsewhere, Patton—who had previously refused to integrate his troops—called on the 761st. In the autumn of 1944, Patton welcomed the African American troops and reminded them that they had a great deal to fight for:

The waterfront was destroyed during the deadly explosion at Port Chicago in July 1944.

"Men, you're the first Negro tankers to ever fight in the American Army. I would never have asked for you if you weren't good. I have nothing but the best in my Army ... Everyone has their eyes on you and is expecting great things from you. Most of all your race is looking forward to you. Don't let them down and damn you, don't let me down!"[38] The 761st did not let anyone down. They performed heroically, earning more than 60 Bronze Stars, 11 Silver Stars, and 280 Purple Hearts.

As World War II came to an end, it was clear that some progress had been made for African Americans. Black troops were able to engage in combat, but the irony of their fighting Germany and its discrimination and violence against the Jewish race was not lost on them. As Stephen Ambrose wrote in *Citizen Soldier*, "The world's greatest democracy fought the world's greatest racist with a segregated army."[39] One "V" for victory—that against Hitler—had been achieved, but the second "V," for racial equality, was still out of reach.

CHAPTER FIVE
TIME TO
"DO SOMETHING"

The world was at peace once again, but the battle for civil rights was only getting started. The Ku Klux Klan was stronger than ever, and black veterans were still being beaten and lynched, just as had happened after World War I. Local law enforcement was often complicit, as became clear during an incident in South Carolina. A black sergeant named Isaac Woodard was returning home from Fort Gordon, Georgia, when the bus driver scolded him for taking too long in the "colored only" men's bathroom. The driver called the local sheriff to arrest Woodard. Even though the sergeant did not resist arrest, he was still so severely beaten that he was blinded.

Harry Truman, the new president, believed he had understood the extent of racism that black Americans faced, but this incident shocked him. "My God," he said. "I had no idea it was as terrible as that. We've got to do something!"[40]

Backward Steps

The problems faced by African American veterans were not limited to physical violence. After the war, military leaders were rethinking the use of black troops, threatening to wipe out the gains blacks had made during World War II. Although many blacks had served with distinction at the front, their heroics were ignored. Once more, military leaders wanted to restrict the roles and positions open to black enlistees, limiting them to service and labor positions.

African Americans were also excluded from a number of federal programs established to support veterans. Community organizations such as the American Legion and Veterans of Foreign Wars (VFW), with posts in cities and towns throughout the country, were designated "white only," although blacks were sometimes issued limited memberships in separate facilities.

Other programs were difficult for blacks to use simply because of segregation in society as a whole. The G.I. Bill was a prime example. One provision of the bill was to provide money to help veterans pay for college, but this was often useless to blacks because few universities accepted black students. In addition, the strict segregation of neighborhoods meant that G.I. loans for black veterans to use for purchasing a home could be used only in all-black communities.

Political Moves

Although Truman had spoken of his support of civil rights, he was first and foremost a politician, wary to commit to any course of action that could cost him votes in the upcoming 1948 presidential election. He tackled discrimination in the U.S. military only when he believed that a large bloc of black voters in the northern states would vote against him if he did not. On July 26, 1948, Truman issued Executive Order 9981, calling for an end to segregation in all branches of the military:

It is essential that there be maintained in the armed service of the United States the highest standards of democracy, with equality of treatment and opportunity for all those who serve in our country's defense. It is hereby the policy of the President that there shall be equality of treatment and opportunity for all persons in the armed forces, without regard to race, color, religion, or national origin.[41]

To oversee the progress of each of the military branches, Truman set up the Committee on Equality of Treatment and Opportunity in the Armed Forces, headed by former diplomat Charles Fahy. The Fahy Commission regularly reported to the president about the progress, and problems, with implementing the order.

Slow Changes

While the African American community praised Executive Order 9981, most military leaders did not. Some, like General Dwight D. Eisenhower, felt that it was impossible to combat prejudice with an executive order. Other commanders were concerned about the cohesiveness of military units. They worried that integrating soldiers' living, eating, and working conditions would disrupt the unity

President Truman signed Executive Order 9981 to formally end military segregation.

and camaraderie between troops, causing a dangerous distraction during combat. Despite their objections, the military branches had no choice but to follow the president's order.

Since the executive order did not specify an exact timeline for integration, individual military leaders could decide how quickly—or slowly—to implement it. Julius Becton Jr., a 21-year-old officer in training when the order was announced, recalls vividly the attitude of his superior officer: "I remember the post commander assembled all the officers and he read the order to the assembled group. He then said, 'As long as I am commander here, there will be no change.'"[42]

The pace of integration varied from branch to branch. The air force quickly ended its restrictions on the number of blacks allowed to enlist and announced that troops would be assigned duties based on their abilities, not their skin color. Within a year, the number of African Americans in the air force increased by nearly 500 men each month. The navy, too, opened up more spots for black enlistees, although it was slow to move them away from mess attendant jobs.

The Marine Corps and the army were far more resistant to making changes. Their leaders were more outspoken about what they saw as the dangers of integration. Both branches fell short of the goals and did not make much progress in integrating either training or living facilities.

When the integration process finally did speed up, it was not because of Truman or Fahy, but because—once again—of war. On June 25, 1950, the Communist government of North Korea invaded South Korea. Since the United States was vehement in its condemnation of communism, Truman ordered American troops to help the South Koreans repel the invasion. Commanders at training bases throughout the United States soon found themselves overrun with untrained young men. They did not have the luxury of time in getting the recruits ready to fight, so it was a far more efficient use of space to integrate the training and living facilities.

Integration at Last

Of course, even the outside pressures of war did not make desegregation a smooth or uncontroversial process. Some field commanders were resolutely against integration and knew that the Fahy Commission could do little about it if they chose to continue segregating troops in faraway

In October 1950, President Truman (bottom left) met with (clockwise from top left) American secretary of state Dean Acheson, U.S. general George Marshall, and English prime minister Clement Attlee to discuss the situation in Korea.

Korea. For the most part, however, whites and blacks fought alongside one another, and for the first time in U.S. history, black officers commanded white soldiers.

Charles Armstrong, a black army sergeant during the Korean War, found himself in command of white soldiers. "Some used the 'n' word, but I got over it," he recalled. One white soldier used the word repeatedly until another white soldier in his troop corrected him. "He told him I was an officer and not to do that to me," he said. "That guy became one of my best soldiers." In the end, Armstrong said, the men realized they needed him, and that resulted in respect. "My job was being a combat officer," he recalled later. "I led the troops into combat ... The white soldiers ... realized they had to follow me if they wanted to get out alive."[43]

The Korean War lasted for three years, and although it produced decidedly mixed results politically, it was a positive beginning to the integration of the armed forces. For example, the African American presence in the Marine Corps increased from 1,075 to 15,000. The air force abandoned its policy of creating all-black fighter squadrons and instead began assigning black pilots wherever they were needed. The army,

too, underwent a transformation, with 92 percent of black soldiers serving in integrated units.

In the years following the Korean War, the civil rights movement in the United States grew stronger. Leaders such as Dr. Martin Luther King Jr. helped organize protests to fight discrimination in education, housing, and employment, especially in the South, where Jim Crow was still very much in practice.

By then, the military was the most integrated institution in the nation. Even though military pay was no way to get rich, the armed forces provided steady work and allowed black soldiers to learn skills that could potentially lead to higher-paying jobs in civilian life later. There were many opportunities for blacks to advance, so it was not surprising that the number of blacks in uniform increased after the Korean War rather than diminished.

The War in Vietnam

While integration had largely been achieved, the next war would bring new challenges. The United States entered the jungles of South Vietnam for the same reason it got involved with Korea: to fight

In 1966, President Lyndon B. Johnson went to Fort Campbell in Kentucky to meet soldiers stationed there.

communism. By the late 1950s, President Dwight D. Eisenhower, among others, feared that Communist North Vietnam could take control of South Vietnam, bringing the world one step closer to global communism.

At first, U.S. involvement was limited to providing South Vietnam with financial support and about 700 military advisors who went to the country to help organize and train the South Vietnamese army. However, it soon became apparent that the South Vietnamese were not prepared to fight the North alone. By the latter part of 1964, the United States had sent about 100,000 troops into the Vietnam War.

For the first time in history, the percentage of black troops in Vietnam was nearly the same as that of the black population of the United States—about 10 percent. They served in virtually every capacity and were awarded medals and promotions in numbers that far surpassed what blacks had received in previous wars.

Such progress was heartening to black troops in Vietnam. Lieutenant Colonel George Shaffer, one of the highest-ranking black officers in the army, said, "I feel good about it. Not that I like bloodshed, but the performance of the Negro in Vietnam tends to offset the fact that the Negro wasn't considered worthy of being a front-line officer in other wars."[44]

Fighting for Whose Rights?

As the presence of U.S. troops in Vietnam expanded, President Lyndon B. Johnson, who took office in 1963, assured the American people that the troops were there only to assist the South Vietnamese and that the war would be brief.

This optimistic outlook proved wrong. The war dragged on, and the American public grew increasingly frustrated. The war seemed to have little to do with the United States, but tens of thousands of American soldiers were being killed—with no end in sight. African American leaders especially criticized U.S. involvement in the conflict. Dr. Martin Luther King Jr. noted that the military was sending young black men to fight for democracy and rights that they were being denied at home. "[W]e have been repeatedly faced with the cruel irony of watching Negro and white boys on TV screens," he said, "as they kill and die together for a nation that has been unable to seat them together in the same school."[45]

More militant voices insisted

As the Vietnam War went on, the number of black men being drafted to fight was called into question, as can be seen on this protest button.

UGLY WORDS

In her book *We Were There: Voices of African American Veterans, from World War II to the War in Iraq*, Yvonne Latty included an interview with James Brantley, who served in Vietnam. Brantley recalled his shock at the racism he encountered in Vietnam—not by whites, but by the people he was there to help:

> *When I first got to Saigon one of the first things I saw was this tooth-paste advertisement prominently placed. It was called "Light Bright" or something, and they had this little caricature of a black man, something you would see in the South, the Sambo thing. This guy is smiling with big white teeth, and that impacted me. I knew how they saw blacks based on that ad. In South Vietnam you could hear the young kids calling us [an offensive word for black people]. Someone else taught them that word. It wasn't a word from their culture, yet it seemed to pop up at times. I was in a bar one night and heard a Vietnamese citizen scream out [the same offensive word] to a black GI. It was chilling, upsetting. An argument broke out after that between the two men. I had to try and stay calm, but it was hard. That ugly word was what white GIs brought to the Vietnamese people. It was not their hateful language—it was ours.[1]*

1. Quoted in Yvonne Latty, *We Were There: Voices of African American Veterans, from World War II to the War in Iraq*. New York, NY: Amistad, 2004, pp. 121–123.

that because the U.S. government did not guarantee or protect black civil rights, blacks should not be drafted into the armed forces at all. One group, the Black Panther Party for Self-Defense, demanded that all black men should be exempt from military service, saying, "We will not fight and kill other people of color in the world who, like black people, are being victimized by the white racist government of America."[46]

As more and more young men were drafted for the Vietnam War, the ratio of black troops to white grew significantly. Many African Americans who had enlisted early on chose to reenlist, often because they knew that being a soldier was a better job than they could hope for in the discriminatory civilian world.

When the war intensified, however, there was a more sinister reason for the high proportion of blacks. Increasing numbers of young men were required to report to their local draft boards. In the South, those draft boards were almost exclusively white. In the past, Southern draft boards had found excuses to exclude African Americans from the armed forces. Now, those same draft boards were doing the opposite, drafting 64 percent of eligible black men, compared to just 31 percent of eligible white men.

This time around, many white soldiers were assigned to technical and support duties—behind the lines—while the vast majority of black troops went to the front as infantry. Ironically, the combat duty sought by black soldiers in other wars as a means to prove their worth was not as desirable in Vietnam, because guerrilla warfare and frequent ambushes meant there was a higher risk of being killed. Not surprisingly, during much of the war, black soldiers died at a higher rate than white soldiers. Many blacks pointed to the injustice of bearing more than their share of the burden of the war.

Violence at Home

One evening, Dr. Martin Luther King Jr. stood on the balcony of his hotel room in Memphis, Tennessee, looking out over the city and thinking about how best to share his message of peace. Suddenly, at 6:01 p.m., a single bullet brought an abrupt end to it all. King was assassinated on April 4, 1968, by James Earl Ray, an escaped criminal. The impact of the murder rippled throughout the world. Riots broke out across the United States, and for many black soldiers, Dr. King's death was the breaking point.

In Vietnam, black soldiers held protests after King's murder only to be met with taunting by some white troops. Author Michael Herr, who served in Vietnam, wrote, "The death of Martin Luther King intruded on the war in a way that no other outside event had ever done. In the days that followed, there were a number of small, scattered riots, one or two stabbings, all of it denied officially."[47]

While incidents such as these had a divisive effect, the troops were united by a belief they all shared: No one thought the Vietnam War could be won. Soldiers were not sure why they were even there. Americans were largely against the war, and

Following the assassination of Martin Luther King Jr., many African Americans took to the streets to march in protest.

this negative public opinion weighed heavily on the troops. When they did return to the United States, some people called them names, spit on them, and threatened them. For the first time, the skin color of these soldiers was irrelevant. They were bound together by the fact that many of their own countrymen despised them.

CHAPTER SIX
DEALING WITH INJUSTICE

African Americans' demands for civil rights exploded after the assassination of Martin Luther King Jr., and racial tension among troops was only one problem. Another issue, growing uglier by the day, was the country's draft system. While it had been used for years to supply the needed troops in the war, it now proved insufficient, and the military did not have enough qualified soldiers. Draft boards allowed deferments, or delays of service, for college and graduate students, and President Johnson knew that if those deferments were revoked, it would anger middle- and upper-class voters. As a solution, the president's secretary of defense, Robert McNamara, came up with another idea—and it would not affect those deferments.

New Approaches

McNamara's idea was to enlist the men who previously had been rejected for not meeting the military's physical or mental requirements. Recruiters visited poor neighborhoods and the backcountry roads of southern towns, enlisting all willing young men. A little more than 40 percent of the new recruits were black— almost four times the percentage of blacks in the overall U.S. population.

Many of these recruits, both black and white, had emotional problems, anger issues, and learning disabilities. Many, too, had drug and alcohol addictions that only worsened during their time in Vietnam. A large percentage were incapable of taking and following orders—leading to an unkind nickname, the "Moron Corps," which veteran soldiers used to describe the new recruits. Although McNamara had originally promised that the new recruits would be taught technological skills to help them obtain decent jobs following their service, in reality, most were trained only for combat and assigned to the infantry on the front lines.

It was little wonder that government and military leaders began formulating new ways to rebuild the military after the Vietnam War ended. One of their first steps was to eliminate the draft in 1973. This ended both the practice of giving deferments and of having hostile troops who did not want to serve in the first place. The Department of Defense announced plans for the All-Volunteer Force (AVF). Knowing that, in the past, African Americans had been both over- and underrepresented, Secretary of Defense Melvin Land stressed that the new military goal was to attract young men and women of character, regardless of race or ethnicity. "We do not foresee any significant difference between

THE CHANGE OF A CENTURY

In 1918, during World War I, Private Walter Beagles, a new African American draftee, arrived at Camp Jackson in South Carolina. As part of a segregated army, he was put to work loading and unloading ships, building roads, and digging ditches. He was later deployed to France and was honorably discharged when the war ended. Beagles died in 1985 at the age of 94. A century later, his great-grandson, Brigadier Milford Beagle Jr., serves as commanding general of Camp Jackson.

"It does become pretty surreal to know that the gates my great-grandfather came through are the same gates I come through," stated Beagle. "You always reflect back to you're standing on somebody's shoulders. Somebody put that stair in place so you can move one more rung up ... Somebody at some point in time said your particular race can't do that," he continued. "At some point our ancestors fought so we could be in those front-line units and those combat units." When asked what he might say if he had the chance to see his great-grandfather one more time, the commander replied, "I would turn to him and say, hey, was it worth it," Beagle confided. "And I'm pretty sure I'd get a big smile back and he'd say it was absolutely worth it."[1]

1. Quoted in Christina L. Myers, "General's Family: From Segregation to Command in 100 Years," Associated Press, March 16, 2019. www.apnews.com/cb4ebe64c0f14c30aabc62ba493766f5.

the racial composition of the All-Volunteer Force and the racial composition of the nation," he said shortly before the AVF began. "We are determined that the All-Volunteer Force shall have a broad appeal to young men and women of all racial, ethnic, and economic backgrounds."[48]

To attract what they frequently referred to as "the best and the brightest," recruiters swarmed to U.S. college campuses to talk to students. The Reserve Officers Training Corps, or ROTC, was expanded and improved. For the first time, African American colleges and universities had ROTC programs. High schools with predominantly black or Latinx student bodies offered junior ROTC programs to train teens in drills and military procedures and make a future in the military a more likely option.

These members of a high school ROTC program participated in a drill competition in 1969. ROTC programs continue to be part of schools across the United States.

Television commercials encouraged young people to "be all that you can be" by joining the military. Pay scales for every rank were increased, and more educational opportunities were offered as ways to entice recruits. By 1975, these efforts were so successful that every person in the military was a volunteer.

Success Stories

Of course, racism in the military had not disappeared. Neither executive orders nor nationwide civil rights battles could overcome such a deep-rooted problem. It was an enormous challenge to try to get people to abandon—or at least manage—the biases they had grown up with. In response, in 1971, the military instituted a zero tolerance policy regarding racist behavior from its officers. Anyone who felt like they could not set aside their prejudices was advised to retire quickly. Some did, and those who remained worked to become more racially sensitive by taking seminars and reading training materials. Each unit was required to have a race-relations council. Its job was to consider complaints and arbitrate any problems that arose.

During the post-Vietnam era, the military focused on promoting black soldiers at the same rate as their white counterparts. Finally, talented black soldiers were recognized and rewarded for their services. One of these was Daniel "Chappie" James Jr., who had been a vocal opponent of segregation in the military during World War II, when he participated in a sit-in against white-only officers' clubs. Although the military frowned on this action, during the Korean War, James's abilities as a fighter pilot were highly valued. He received the Distinguished Service Cross and went on to become the first black airman to lead an integrated fighter squadron. After flying more than 160 combat missions in Korea and Vietnam, James became the first African American four-star general in U.S. history.

Another first was the promotion of General Fred Gordon, who was appointed the first African American commandant of cadets at West Point in 1987. Gordon had fought bravely during two tours in Vietnam and served as an army liaison to Congress. Coincidentally, his promotion occurred exactly 100 years after Henry O. Flipper became the first black graduate of West Point.

An even bigger first took place with Nadja West. She grew up in a military family, with her father and nine of her older siblings serving. She

Even after struggling for equality in the military, Daniel James Jr. said that if given another chance, he would still join the air force.

knew she would enlist and hoped to use her love of science in her job. A big fan of Spock from *Star Trek*, she said, "I wanted to be a Vulcan. And I wanted to be a scientist."[49] West attended the U.S. Military Academy at West Point and then went to medical school. By 1990, she was serving as a captain in the Persian Gulf War. By 2015, she had become surgeon general of the entire U.S. Army. Today, she is the army's first black, female three-star general. As the *Washington Post* stated, "Mr. Spock would be proud."[50]

A Man of Note

One of the most famous African American soldiers in history is General Colin Powell, who rose through the ranks of the army to the top military position in the nation—chairman of the Joint Chiefs of Staff (JCS). The JCS is a panel of the highest-ranking officers of each of the military branches. As chairman from 1989 to 1993, Powell became the main military advisor to the president and to the secretary of defense.

Powell had served two tours of duty in Vietnam, where he received a medal for rescuing

Colin Powell (center) was an important figure in the American military and in politics for many years.

SEPTEMBER 11

Major Anthony LaSure was part of the 177th Fighter Wing stationed in New Jersey in 2001. In this excerpt from Yvonne Latty's *We Were There: Voices of African American Veterans, from World War II to the War in Iraq*, LaSure recalls the morning of September 11, 2001, when terrorists attacked multiple locations in the United States. He remembers his mission that day—and for months afterwards—was to prevent more attacks:

On September 11, I was ... scheduled to fly to Fort Drum, New York, to pick up bombs and do some live exercises. I remember it like it was yesterday. It was this bright, clear morning—it was crystal clear. I thought, this is going to be such a nice day to fly. We were all on the runway taxiing and all of a sudden I got this call to come back in. Right away I think, Oh, my God, something's happened to someone's kid, because this has never happened before ...

The chief came up to us and said a plane just rammed into the World Trade Center ... Then [on television] we saw the second plane crash and we got permission to take off, heading toward New York ...

It was the scariest thing. The Northeast corridor is the busiest airspace in the country, probably the world ... It's hard to get a word in edgewise as far as traffic control goes, and procedures are tight. But we took off that day and our Guard fighter planes could fly any altitude we wanted to at any airspeed. My wingman and I flew fourteen hours that day; it was a long day. We were intercepting airplanes and everyone was told to land. We were going after stragglers ... No one knew what was going on.

While I was flying, I compartmentalized. I didn't have time to think about the attacks or the lives that were lost ... For three months straight I only had twelve hours off, a day to go home, see my family, and sleep. This had never been done before—patrolling our own country.[1]

1. Quoted in Yvonne Latty, *We Were There: Voices of African American Veterans, from World War II to the War in Iraq.* New York, NY: Amistad, 2004, p. 167.

fellow soldiers from a helicopter crash. A strong and capable commanding officer, Powell was even more effective as a military advisor. He worked in Washington and at the Pentagon for many years, helping bridge the gap between politicians and the military. Powell became the highly recognizable face of the Persian Gulf War in 1991, when he held numerous press briefings to explain what was happening in the Middle East.

In 2001, Powell was appointed by President George W. Bush to be secretary of state. At that time, this was the highest government rank ever held by an African American. He stayed in the position until 2005. During his years of service, Powell was awarded two Presidential Medals of Freedom and worked as chairman of America's Promise: The Alliance for Youth, an organization devoted to helping young people become successful adults.

Powell dedicated much of his life to his country and to helping African Americans. As he wrote in his autobiography, *My American Journey*, "There was only one way to reduce the proportion of blacks in the military: let the rest of American society open its doors to African-Americans and give them the opportunity they now enjoyed in the armed forces."[51]

An Ongoing Issue

The American military has continued to work hard to eradicate racial discrimination, and today, African Americans serve in all its branches, in every capacity, and at all ranks. However, racism is an issue that plagues society as a whole, and despite efforts to combat it, bias still exists in the military. For example, a 2017 study from a military advocacy group showed that black soldiers are more likely than white soldiers to be punished or disciplined for infractions. As retired Colonel Don Christenson stated, white soldiers who have done something wrong "probably get the benefit of the doubt that the African American males don't."[52]

A spokesman from the Pentagon stated that, "It is longstanding Department of Defense policy that service members must be afforded the opportunity to serve in an environment free from unlawful racial discrimination."[53] However, according to the 2017 report and a number of experts, "The military's own data raises serious challenges to the idea that the system in its current form is capable of delivering impartial justice."[54]

As people lose their biases, the U.S. military will continue to embrace the bravery of its African American troops.

Change is happening—but it happens slowly. John E. James Jr., who graduated from the Army's Officer Candidate School in 1942, was denied his promotion because he was black. He could not be put into a position above white soldiers. Years later, his daughter, Marian Lane, found an old photo of her father from his days in World War II. She had not even known he had served. When she showed him the photo, he told her to throw it away, but Lane had other ideas.

In 2015, she began petitioning the army to change her father's military record. It wasn't easy. She kept running into red tape, and after three years, a dozen emails and letters, and several dead-ends and rejections, she almost gave up. Finally, however, in 2018, the army agreed it was time to make James a second lieutenant. At the age of 98, James put on his uniform and went to the Museum of the American Revolution to take the officer's oath. As Lane put it, "I just felt that my father deserved it. We live in a country where, yes, there are injustices that can happen. We are blessed to be in a country where injustice can also be rectified."[55]

With each passing year, hopefully, injustices will be rectified both in and out of the military. It will take time, patience, and determination, but one day, the United States can be a place where all men and women are created equal.

NOTES

Introduction: Second-Class Citizens

1. Quoted in Jack D. Foner, *Blacks and the Military in American History: A New Perspective*. New York, NY: Praeger Publishers, 1974, p. viii.

Chapter One: Liberty for All?

2. Quoted in Kai Wright, *Soldiers of Freedom: An Illustrated History of African Americans in the Armed Forces*. New York, NY: Black Dog & Leventhal, 2002, p. 8.

3. Quoted in Gail Buckley, *American Patriots: The Story of Blacks in the Military from the Revolution to Desert Storm*. New York, NY: Random House, 2001, pp. 11–12.

4. Quoted in Michael Lee Lanning, *The African-American Soldier: From Crispus Attucks to Colin Powell*. New York, NY: Citadel Press, 2004, p. 8.

5. Quoted in Michael Lee Lanning, *Defenders of Liberty: African American Soldiers in the Revolutionary War*. New York, NY: Citadel Press, 2000, p. 47.

6. Quoted in Buckley, *American Patriots*, p. 14.

7. Quoted in Ray Raphael, *A People's History of the American Revolution: How Common People Shaped the Fight for Independence*. New York, NY: New Press, 2001, p. 54.

8. Quoted in Lanning, *The African-American Soldier*, p. 12.

9. Quoted in "The First Rhode Island Regiment of the Continental Line," AmericanRevolution.org, accessed on April 29, 2019. www.americanrevolution.org/firstri.php.

10. Quoted in Raphael, *A People's History of the American Revolution*, p. 287.

Chapter Two: A Personal Stake

11. Quoted in Buckley, *American Patriots*, p. 80.

12. Quoted in Wright, *Soldiers of Freedom*, p. 60.

13. Quoted in Lanning, *The African-American Soldier*, p. 35.

14. Quoted in Lanning, *The African-American Soldier*, p. 35.

15. Quoted in Foner, *Blacks and the Military*, p. 34.

16. Quoted in Wright, *Soldiers of Freedom*, p. 60.

17. Quoted in Lanning, *The African-American Soldier*, p. 40.

18. Quoted in Lanning, *The African-American Soldier*, pp. 46–47.

19. Quoted in James M. McPherson, *The Negro's Civil War: How American Blacks Felt and Acted During the War for the Union*. New York, NY: Knopf Doubleday, 2003, p. 194.

20. Quoted in Buckley, *American Patriots*, p. 98.

Chapter Three: The World at War

21. Quoted in Wright, *Soldiers of Freedom*, p. 114.

22. Quoted in John Simkin, "Afro-American Soldiers," Spartacus Educational, last updated March 2015. spartacus-educational.com/FWWafro.htm.

23. Quoted in Bernard C. Nalty, *Strength for the Fight: A History of Black Americans in the Military*. New York, NY: Free Press, 1986, p. 107.

24. Quoted in Foner, *Blacks and the Military*, p. 117.

25. Quoted in Foner, *Blacks and the Military*, p. 117.

26. Quoted in Gerald Astor, *The Right to Fight: A History of African Americans in the Military*. Novato, CA: Presidio, 1998, pp. 114–115.

27. Quoted in Buckley, *American Patriots*, p. 173.

28. Quoted in Arthur W. Little, *From Harlem to the Rhine: The Story of New York's Colored Volunteers*. New York, NY: Covici, Friede, 1936, p. 350.

29. Little, *From Harlem to the Rhine*, p. 362.

30. Quoted in Chad Williams, "African-American Veterans Hoped their Service in World War I Would Secure their Rights at Home. It Didn't," *TIME*, November 12, 2018. time.com/5450336/african-american-veterans-wwi/.

31. W.E.B. Du Bois, "Returning Soldiers," Teaching American History, accessed on May 15, 2019. teachingamericanhistory.org/library/document/returning-soldiers/.

32. Quoted in Lanning, *The African-American Soldier*, p. 151.

33. Quoted in Arthur E. Barbeau and Florette Henri, *The Unknown Soldiers: African-American Troops in World War I*. Philadelphia, PA: Temple University Press, 1974, p. 174.

Chapter Four: Working for a Double Victory

34. Quoted in Wright, *Soldiers of Freedom*, p. 155.

35. Quoted in Buckley, *American Patriots*, p. 257.

36. Quoted in Astor, *The Right to Fight*, p. 184.

37. Quoted in Foner, *Blacks and the Military*, p. 147.

38. Quoted in "The 761st Tank Battalion," Black History in America, accessed on May 17, 2019. www.myblackhistory.net/761st.htm.

39. Quoted in "African Americans in World War II: Fighting for a Double Victory," National WWII Museum, accessed on May 17, 2019. www.nationalww2museum.org/sites/default/files/2017-07/african-americans.pdf.

Chapter Five: Time to "Do Something"

40. Quoted in William E. Leuchtenburg, "The Conversion of Harry Truman," *American Heritage*, vol. 42, no. 7, November 1991. www.americanheritage.com/conversion-harry-truman.

41. Quoted in Lanning, *The African-American Soldier*, p. 221.

42. Quoted in Yvonne Latty, *We Were There: Voices of African American Veterans, from World War II to the War in Iraq*. New York, NY: Amistad, 2004, p. 77.

43. Quoted in Latty, *We Were There*, p. 58.

44. Quoted in Foner, *Blacks and the Military*, p. 205.

45. Quoted in Lanning, *The African-American Soldier*, p. 256.

46. Quoted in Wright, *Soldiers of Freedom*, p. 226.

47. Quoted in Buckley, *American Patriots*, p. 409.

Chapter Six: Dealing with Injustice

48. Quoted in Lanning, *The African-American Soldier*, p. 277.

49. Quoted in Marylou Tousignant, "African Americans Long Fought for the Right to Serve their Country," *Washington Post*, February 12, 2018. www.washingtonpost.com/lifestyle/kidspost/african-americans-long-fought-for-the-right-to-serve-their-country/2018/02/12/e38802a6-0768-11e8-b48c-b07fea957bd5_story.html.

50. Tousignant, "African Americans Long Fought."

51. Colin Powell, *My American Journey*. New York, NY: Ballantine Books, 2003, p. 501.

52. Quoted in Carla Herreria, "Even in the Military, Black People are Punished Disproportionately, Report Shows" *HuffPost*, June 7, 2017. www.huffingtonpost.com/entry/study-shoes-black-service-members-punishedmore-in-military_us_5938847ce4b0b13f2c66da83.

53. Quoted in Herreria, "Even in the Military."

54. Quoted in Herreria, "Even in the Military."

55. Quoted in Rachel L. Swarns, "At 98, the Army Just Made Him an Officer: A Tale of Racial Bias in World War II," *New York Times*, June 29, 2018. www.nytimes.com/2018/06/29/us/army-racial-discrimination-african-american-soldier.html.

FOR MORE INFORMATION

Books

Cornell, Kari A. *African Americans in the Civil War*. Minneapolis, MN: Essential Library, 2017.
This book uses photographs and primary sources to enhance the study of how African Americans were involved in the Civil War.

Farrell, Mary Cronk. *Standing Up Against Hate: How Black Women in the Army Helped Change the Course of WWII*. New York, NY: Harry Abrams, 2019.
This book explores the women who joined the military during World War II and how they coped with bias against their race and their gender.

Micklos, John. *Harlem Hellfighters: African-American Heroes of World War I*. North Mankato, MN: Capstone Press, 2017.
Readers get a close-up look at the 369th Regiment during World War I and its pivotal role in important battles.

Miller, Derek L. *Minority Soldiers Fighting in the Korean War*. New York, NY: Cavendish Square, 2018.
This book examines the experience of a variety of minorities during the years of the Korean War.

Randolph, Joanne. *African American Soldiers*. New York, NY: Enslow Publishing, 2018.
This book profiles important African American soldiers throughout history, showing the impact they had on their time period.

Reeder, Eric. *Minority Soldiers Fighting in the American Revolution*. New York, NY: Cavendish Square, 2018.
This book looks at the experience of African Americans before, during, and after the American Revolution.

Sheinkin, Steve. *The Port Chicago 50: Disaster, Mutiny, and the Fight for Civil Rights*. New York, NY: Roaring Brook Press, 2017.
Explore the story of the 50 African American sailors who were convicted of mutiny in 1944.

Websites

National Archives

www.archives.gov/research/alic/ reference/military/blacks-in-military.html
Articles and photo collections housed at the National Archives highlight different aspects of African Americans in the military.

Military.com: African-American Heroism in the Military

www.military.com/history/ african-american-heroism-in-the-military
This web page discusses African Americans' heroic contributions to U.S. war efforts over the centuries. Numerous links point readers to videos, biographical sketches, and more in-depth information.

PBS: African-Americans in Combat

www.pbs.org/opb/ historydetectives/feature/ african-americans-in-combat/
PBS offers this episode as part of its *History Detectives Special Investigations* show, as well as links to different episodes for further information.

Smithsonian Institution's National Museum of African American History and Culture

nmaahc.si.edu/explore/blog
Search the Smithsonian's blog for posts on the African American military experience.

INDEX

PICTURE CREDITS

ABOUT THE AUTHOR

Tamra Orr is the author of more than 500 nonfiction/educational books for readers of all ages. She graduated from Ball State University in Muncie, Indiana, with a degree in English and Education. She planned on becoming an English teacher. Instead, she moved to Oregon and began writing books. She has been fascinated by all elements of history for years and appreciates the chance to explore and discover more about different time periods and important figures in it.